Dedicated to Jazmynn, Baxter, Ciarra, and Willow. :)

Readers Are Leaders Book Series
An imprint of Heritage Press
Beaverton, Oregon

Text copyright © 2016 by Betsie Lewis.
Illustrations copyright © 2016 Heritage Press.

Heritage Press appreciates copyright protections.
To continue to bring you the best books for readers and learners,
we appreciate that you purchased an authorized copy of this book series.
Your purchase helps support future publications
of books just like this one, for your reading pleasure.
Thank you for respecting the copyright of this work
and not scanning, reproducing, copying, or selling any part of this work
without permission from Heritage Press.
We appreciate your help.

my alphabet animals

by Betsie Lewis

HERITAGE PRESS

It's time to learn the alphabet

This is a special book

Because you try to guess what's next

Before you take a look...

...what is next

A is for Alligator
A says "ă, ă, ă"

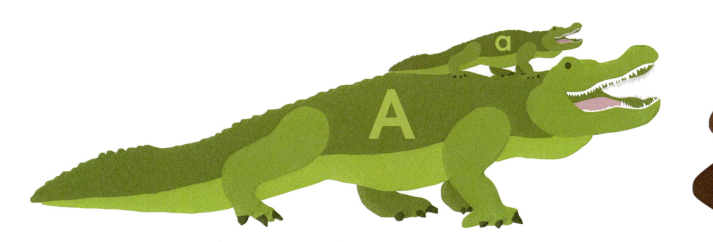

B is for Bear
B says "b, b, b"

C is for Cat
C says "c, c, c"

D is for Dog
D says "d, d, d"

E is for Elephant
E says "ĕ, ĕ, ĕ"

F is for Fox
F says "f, f, f"

G is for Gorilla
G says "g, g, g"

H is for Hippo
H says "h, h, h"

I is for Iguana
I says "ĭ, ĭ, ĭ"

J is for Jellyfish
J says "j, j, j"

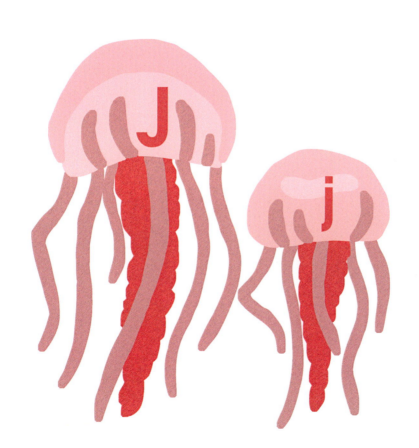

K is for Kangaroo
K says "k, k, k"

L is for Lion
L says "l, l, l"

M is for Moose
M says "m, m, m"

N is for Nightingale
N says "n, n, n"

O is for Ostrich
O says "ŏ, ŏ, ŏ"

P is for Pig
P says "p, p, p"

Q is for Quail
Q says "q, q, q"

R is for Rabbit
R says "r, r, r"

S is for Skunk
S says "s, s, s"

T is for Turtle
T says "t, t, t"

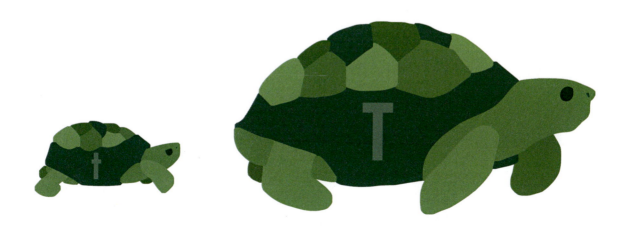

U is for Umbrellabird
U says "ŭ, ŭ, ŭ"

V is for Vulture
V says "v, v, v"

W is for Walrus
W says "w, w, w"

X is for X-ray fish
X says "x, x, x"

Y is for Yak
Y says "y, y, y"

Z is for Zebra
Z says "z, z, z"

Made in the USA
San Bernardino, CA
22 March 2017